THIS JOURNAL BELONGS TO:

_____

THE DIVINE FEMININE JOURNAL

INSPIRING PROMPTS AND PRACTICES
TO RECONNECT TO THE
WISDOM, POWER, AND ENERGY WITHIN

ALISHA J. FLECKY

ROCKRIDGE
PRESS

For general information on our other products and services or to obtain technical support, please contact our Customer Care Department within the United States at (866) 744-2665, or outside the United States at (510) 253-0500.

Rockridge Press publishes its books in a variety of electronic and print formats. Some content that appears in print may not be available in electronic books, and vice versa.

TRADEMARKS: Rockridge Press and the Rockridge Press logo are trademarks or registered trademarks of Callisto Media Inc. and/or its affiliates, in the United States and other countries, and may not be used without written permission. All other trademarks are the property of their respective owners. Rockridge Press is not associated with any product or vendor mentioned in this book.

Interior and Cover Designer: Angela Navarra
Art Producer: Sara Feinstein
Editor: Samantha Holland
Production Editor: Andrew Yackira
Production Manager: Michael Kay

Illustrations used under license from Creative Market

Author photo courtesy of Leanna Flecky

ISBN: Print 978-1-63807-964-4
R0

CONTENTS

Any real ecstasy
is a sign you are moving
in the right direction.

—ST. TERESA OF AVILA
(MYSTIC SAINT; C. 1515–1582)

INTRODUCTION

Welcome! I'm so glad you have chosen to explore and discover your inner divine feminine, and I am honored to move through this journey with you.

The divine feminine is where love dwells inside of you. It is the most sacred part of who you are—your very soul. This place is your inner sanctuary, your connection to others, and the energy of life itself. It is not your outward presentation, but your inner feelings. It feels like your breath being taken away by the stars, your heart opening in compassion for another, your body asking for presence or stillness. Your divine feminine communicates through intuition, synchronicity, and sensation. It is self-nourishing and self-referencing, and it flows like the cycles of the moon. But how can we access it?

Collectively, we have forgotten the simple art of being delighted with the world around us. Many people suffer from modern issues like disconnection from the body, insatiable ambition, and excessive individualism. Burnout, self-criticism, and addiction to approval in society are signs that we have lost touch with ourselves. There is a disconnect from our inner reservoir of connection, self-nourishment, and simple pleasures. We are siphoned off from our own water source, and this desert leaves us disillusioned and thirsty.

The good news is that the tools you need to replenish your water source are available to you. This book offers the grounded, visceral experience of discovering the divine feminine energy that already lives in you. We will journey step-by-step in discovering and nurturing pathways into your inner sanctuary.

In ancient times, worship of the Goddess in her various forms prevailed across the planet, including Kali, Athena, Isis, Freya, Oshun, and Guan Yin, among others. Deep in our bones, the ancient ways stay with us and are still practiced in places today. We hearken back to that era with our yearning for the divine feminine. However, it's important to understand that this book is not associated with any specific Goddess tradition, nor is it meant to supersede any other spiritual beliefs. Instead, it offers tools and reflections that act as a cornerstone and an important first step in sacred feminine work for anyone who wants to tap into its energy. You do not have to adhere to a Goddess tradition to benefit from this book. The aim is self-nourishment and to open pathways to a more enriching and delightful life.

Let this book be a contemplative space of rest and nourishment for you. Read it on a comfy couch, maybe with a pet by your side or a cup of tea. Move through it in whatever way you are inspired; read one page a day or skip around. Do it alone or with trusted friends. There is only one rule: *Don't let this journal become another task on your to-do list.* When you open these pages, do so with the intention of entering into the still quiet of your soul. The more time and space you allow, the deeper and more impactful these lessons will be. Savor them. Write down spontaneous insights. If inspiration arises, follow it. You know your path better than anyone.

This book uses tools such as visualization exercises, journaling, rituals, experiments in mindfulness, and other practices to help one feel at home in their body. These various techniques move us beyond the rational, conceptual mind and into an embodied, intuitive experience. As we gradually deepen into our blood and bones, we learn to surrender to a greater wisdom, power, and beauty that exists within. By the end of this book, I hope you have a visceral sense of these qualities within you.

It's important to note that while a guided journal is a great way to work through complex feelings and understand yourself more deeply, it is not a substitute for therapy. Any ongoing feelings of anxiety or depression should be addressed by a trained medical professional. Seeking therapy is a courageous act of self-care to be applauded and never shamed. See page 159 for therapeutic and healing resources.

My own journey began many years ago on a dark night in the Thai jungle. I was sitting alone on my bungalow balcony, and I felt my heart deeply connect to the jungle at night. A conversation emerged—it happened inside of me, though it was viscerally felt as a divine force outside of myself. I connected to a mysterious and sweet divine feminine voice full of wisdom. It was the first unmistakable conscious experience I had with what I'd call "divine feminine energy."

That experience led me to spend years studying a variety of Goddess practices in India, Thailand, and Brazil. Later, I reintegrated with the West, studying the mind-body connection through somatics, embodiment, mindfulness, psychology, and intergenerational trauma healing. My experiences have helped shape this journal, informed the wisdom behind the prompts and exercises, and will hopefully help bring inspiration and clarity to your divine feminine journey as well.

You don't have to go to the other side of the world to tap into your divine feminine energy. You have it within you right now, and this book will show you how to ignite it. In doing so, you'll discover a place beyond the conditioning of society and bring to light the most authentic and powerful version of yourself.

May the wisdom of your inner sacred space deepen into your bones, light up your heart, and nourish the world around you. Let's begin.

Inside myself is a place where I live all alone and that is where you renew your springs that never dry up.

—PEARL S. BUCK

SECTION 1

AWAKEN THE DIVINE FEMININE WITHIN

The divine feminine is a living current of energy that makes up all life. It lives inside and through all bodies, beings, and places. You awaken to it by relaxing into who you deeply are, not by forcing yourself to "become" an image of it. This journal offers many opportunities to listen to and explore your inner world, where you will discover treasures that are inherently divine.

One way to understand the inner world is through the lens of inner masculine and feminine. I will use these words throughout this section; however, if these words are uncomfortable or charged for you in any way, please feel free to exchange them for "emissive and receptive" or "yang and yin." Even though these energies can be gendered, they exist inside all bodies, regardless of how one identifies.

The exercises and prompts in this section will help you to soften into your inner feminine, feel your feelings, listen to your intuition, and open your heart. By nurturing your inner feminine through these exercises and journal prompts, you'll create space for the divine feminine to awaken.

What called you to pick up this book? What is the outcome you are hoping for? Pause and let your body be still while you seek your answers. Feel the feelings that brought you here. Are you desiring more spirituality in your life or to nourish your feminine side? Do you yearn to experience a feminine form of divinity? Bringing this yearning to the surface will help map your journey ahead.

_____

_____

_____

_____

_____

_____

_____

_____

_____

_____

_____

Let's begin this journey by familiarizing yourself with your inner feminine as she is now. Close your eyes and think of what your inner feminine might be like in human form. No need to overthink it—have some fun envisioning her! Describe her in the space below. What can you learn about yourself from this image?

_____

_____

_____

_____

_____

_____

_____

_____

_____

_____

_____

RITUAL MOVEMENT

Rituals are a powerful way to affect your inner world. When inner experience is represented by outer symbolic movements, a powerful exchange happens that impacts our psyches and strengthens our intentions. Let's start this journey with a ritual. Here are some steps you can follow or use for inspiration:

1. Clear time to be alone, at least 10 to 15 minutes.

2. Light a candle or incense, or perform some other gesture to establish a sacred space.

3. Sit with your eyes closed and take three long, deep breaths.

4. Feel into your yearning to connect with the divine feminine inside you.

5. Make a statement, aloud or silently, that sums up your desire.

6. Bow your head or hold your hand to your heart to complete the ritual.

Find a quiet place to listen deeply to your inner self. Ask yourself, "What do I desire?" and observe what spontaneously arises inside of you. Write your answers down. Keep asking yourself this question and notice as you discover new answers— let them come from a deeper place inside each time. Continue this exercise until you have a clear picture of your heart's desires. What do you long for?

_____

_____

_____

_____

_____

_____

_____

_____

_____

_____

How do you imagine your life would change if your deepest heartfelt desires led the way? Refer to the previous prompt if you need a reminder. Which desires can you put into practice? Describe what your life could be or feel like. How can you start to make this happen? Write about at least one small way you can start today.

_____

_____

_____

_____

_____

_____

_____

_____

_____

_____

DIVINE AWAKENING

What do you imagine your divine feminine awakening will be like? Sometimes, awakening this raw power and beauty within us is like a previously dormant volcano exploding with hot lava; other times, it's a gentle stream weaving through the woods. It can feel like the first burst of sunlight filling the dawn sky or a crack of lightning illuminating unseen places, or it can move at a glacial pace, slowly unveiling who you are.

In the space below or on a separate piece of paper, draw a picture of what your divine feminine awakening might look like using inspiration from the forces of nature—such as volcanoes, waterfalls, jungles, streams, lightning, or galaxies. Close your eyes, take a breath, feel your body, and let an image come to you.

Divine feminine energy is closely intertwined with your own personal current of joy. When was the last time you felt joyful? Any small moment counts. What were you doing in that moment? Write about it and include a description of how it felt. How can you evoke more small moments of joy in your life?

_____

_____

_____

_____

_____

_____

_____

_____

_____

_____

_____

The daily grind of adult life can create blocks that prevent our inner joy from flowing. For most of us, our divine nature was more accessible to us as children. What was your favorite thing to do as a child? What did you love? What was magical to you? Spend some time remembering. How can you experience some of those feelings today?

_____

_____

_____

_____

_____

_____

_____

_____

_____

_____

JOYFUL EXPRESSION

Connecting to joy in our daily lives feeds our souls and rewires our brains toward happiness. We don't always need a reason to be happy. Tomorrow, start your day with some dancing, for no particular reason. Choose a song that fits your mood—something you feel like moving or dancing to. If dancing isn't your thing, you can stand up and walk around or sway while the music plays. Let the music fill you with energy, playfulness, and spontaneity.

If you can, try this practice every day this week. If you like it, make it a daily habit. A little morning movement can transform your day!

Our minds give us endless tasks and goals, even when they're not a true desire of our hearts. Gain some clarity by writing down all the things your mind wants to accomplish. Afterwards, take deep breaths and sit in silence with your hand on your heart or belly for a minute. Review your list and draw a heart next to each goal that feels like an authentic desire of your heart. How can you rewrite your list to reflect more of your heart's deeper desires?

_____

_____

_____

_____

_____

_____

_____

_____

_____

_____

May you realize that
the shape of your soul is
unique, that you have a
special destiny here, that
behind the façade of your
life there is something
beautiful, good, and
eternal happening.

—JOHN O'DONOHUE

By connecting with our subconscious minds, we begin clearing the path to hear divine feminine wisdom. Get in touch by practicing stream-of-consciousness writing. Write down the next thing that you see—for example, "window." Then write the next thing your mind thinks of, like "eyes." Keep going until you fill the page. The words don't need to be related logically—simply let your subconscious flow. Afterwards, look over your page. What can you learn about how your mind works?

WHAT DO YOU FEEL?

We rarely get the chance to do what we *feel*, because we have so many responsibilities and often a strong need to be productive. It's hard to break out of *doing* and switch into *feeling*.

Today, set aside 20 minutes to do whatever you feel. Here's one suggestion, but feel free to follow your own inspiration.

1. Turn off your cell phone, light some candles, and use pillows to support the front and back of your body. Put on soothing music.

2. Relax the body and release your to-do list. Let go of striving, of trying to "become" something.

3. Ask yourself: "What do I really *feel* like doing now?" Notice what your body's yearning and inner inspiration says. Maybe you feel like calling a friend, baking something, or simply sitting in that very spot and reflecting.

4. Trust your inner voice and follow what spontaneously arises. Make this a regular practice to connect with your divine feminine.

14

Developing your inner masculine creates a protective and energetic foundation for your inner feminine to thrive. List what you consider to be your more "masculine" or "yang" traits. Some examples could be a mind for accomplishing goals, ability to act, dynamism, fearlessness, or discipline. Describe how these qualities help you in life. What is your inner masculine like?

_____

_____

_____

_____

_____

_____

_____

_____

_____

_____

Modern life tends to reward "masculine" traits more than "feminine." This imbalance causes exaggeration of our so-called masculine traits. Describe the ways your masculine qualities might be distorted—such as a constant pressure to perform or an inability to process emotions. Our inner masculine needs to build a relationship with the inner feminine, ensuring she is a part of all decisions. How can your feminine soothe your inner masculine? What does he need? How can they work together?

TAKE SPACE FOR YOURSELF

Learning to make space for our sacred feminine takes time and practice. When relating with others, sometimes we get so taken by an impulse—such as the need to respond favorably to a request—that we don't give our deeper feminine a chance to influence our responses. Imagine a triggering moment for you, and practice the following steps ahead of time, so you're prepared for when it happens next.

1. **Pause.** When an impulse to react negatively arises, pause. (Over time, this will get easier.)

2. **Ground and discharge.** Feel your feet beneath you, wiggle your toes, or move your body in a way that feels soothing. This can help discharge reactive energy.

3. **Get spacious.** Rest for a moment. Feel your gut, your heart, your intuition. What is your deeper experience? Your true need? How does your heart want to respond?

4. **Respond.** Step forward and respond from your authentic center.

Imagine a conversation between you and your innermost divine feminine self. You can imagine this self represented by a form of the divine feminine, such as Mother Mary, Guan Yin, Kali, or Isis—or write from the perspective of divine qualities such as "compassion," "love," or "wisdom." Ask questions regarding current themes in your life and listen quietly for an answer. Write down the conversation and any wisdom you discover.

Take a moment to imagine the divine creative principle (you might call this God, spirit, or life energy) as feminine. What would that mean for you personally? We often find that our subconscious is imprinted with the idea that this energy is solely male. Just as an experiment, how would it be to imagine it as female? Would you relate differently? Consider also the nongendered form of spirit. Write down your thoughts as you reflect on this topic.

_____

_____

_____

_____

_____

_____

_____

_____

_____

_____

Divine feminine energy inspires us to embrace all of our selves, including our shadows. Which parts of your self do you want to accept more? Describe these often-hidden or secret parts below. Are they envy, neediness, anger, or fear? Something else? What words of compassion, kindness, or understanding can you give to these parts of yourself without judgment?

_____

_____

_____

_____

_____

_____

_____

_____

_____

_____

_____

MINDFUL MEDITATION

Scrolling social media, multitasking, hopping between roles and activities—our attention is often scattered, and our minds become conditioned by distraction. A meditation or mindfulness practice is a vital tool for self-discovery. This exercise will help purify and relax your busy mind. It is inspired by a classic yogic technique called *trataka*.

1. Light a candle and allow your gaze to rest on the candle for 3 to 5 minutes.

2. Take deep breaths and let your shoulders and belly soften.

3. If any unpleasant thoughts or worries arise, imagine they are being offered to—and dissolved by—the flame.

4. Pay special attention to the area in the center of your forehead, and let your energy accumulate restfully there.

5. Afterwards, notice if you feel calmer or more focused.

If you enjoyed this exercise, make it a routine every morning or evening.

Beauty is an expression of the divine feminine. What do you think is beautiful? Let your heart express its recognition of beauty. You might discover beauty in the strength of a friend, the smell of certain foods, or the colors of the ocean. Expressions of beauty are limitless—the more you find, the more you will see. What other hidden beauties can you recognize in your life?

_____

_____

_____

_____

_____

_____

_____

_____

_____

Devotion is one of the most powerful frequencies of love we can experience as humans. What are you devoted to? It might be specific people, communities, places, animals, or forms of divinity, ideas, or principles, for example. When you are devoted, you feel love, care, and the desire to serve. How do you express devotion? How might you like to express it more?

_____

_____

_____

_____

_____

_____

_____

_____

_____

_____

CREATE A SACRED SPACE

Let's create a sacred space to commemorate your divine feminine journey. Anchoring inner work to an outer reality is an important aspect of the journey. Find an area of your room or home in which you can create a sacred space.

Build a sacred space using a shelf, chair, table, or even a windowsill. Place some objects or photos that represent what this path means to you and what you are calling to you through this book. You might be inspired to write meaningful words on a piece of paper and place it there as well.

Aim to keep this space energetically fresh and beautiful. Place some fresh flowers there or burn a candle in the room. Take time to sit here quietly and reflect on occasion.

As I awaken to
my divine feminine
essence, I surrender
to the beauty of life
within and around me.

This is your body, your greatest gift, pregnant with wisdom you do not hear, grief you thought was forgotten, and joy you have never known.

—MARION WOODMAN

FEEL AT HOME IN YOUR BODY

Your body is a gateway to your deeper nature, your soul, and your divine essence. It can be understood as the literal "house" for your soul and spirit while walking on this Earth. Creating an intimate connection with your body is an essential step in nurturing your divine feminine energy.

Many don't have access to this connection for a variety of reasons—distraction, busyness, lack of education, trauma, or the unhealthy demands of society. The good news is that this connection can be restored.

Let's take time to explore your unique embodied magic and rediscover the joy of being in a body. We'll reflect on imposed beliefs, practice embodiment, open ourselves to pleasure, learn grounding techniques, and more. Through these prompts and exercises, you'll feel more deeply connected to your body and know more about its inherent beauty, wisdom, and power.

How does your body help you? Sometimes we become so focused on changing, controlling, or healing our bodies, we forget to honor how it already serves us. Write about the physiological and emotional ways your body supports you—for example, by digesting food, helping process emotions, and giving us the strength to move. Your body is already miraculous! Reflect on these miracles in the space below.

_____

_____

_____

_____

_____

_____

_____

_____

_____

_____

Make a list of your favorite healthy activities or habits for your body. Some examples might be taking a warm bath, hiking in nature, stretching in the morning, afternoon power naps, or cuddling with a pet. It is so helpful to bring awareness to what you love. Write about how each of these activities makes you feel. See if you can integrate just one extra healthy activity a week into your life.

_____

_____

_____

_____

_____

_____

_____

_____

_____

MINDFUL REST

Rest is an essential part of divine feminine wisdom. Resting gives the body a chance to restore itself and helps soothe and settle emotions. Prepare your body and mind for a restful night's sleep with a relaxing 10-minute body scan.

1. Set a timer for 10 minutes and make yourself very comfortable. Lay down, play relaxing music, light a candle, hug a pillow, support your head, and cozy up in a blanket.

2. Allow for a gradual relaxation of your entire body, starting with your feet and slowly moving up to your head, loosening all parts of your body. Imagine tension draining away or warm honey being poured over your body.

3. Try counting to 4 as you inhale, and counting to 6 as you exhale.

It's okay if you aren't able to fully let go—over time this process will become easier. Keep practicing, and have a good night's sleep!

The most loyal friend you will ever have is your body. Your body will be with you until the very end. What needs of your body have you been ignoring? Looking back on your life so far, in what ways can you improve this relationship? Sit in silence and give your body time to speak. Write a letter to yourself from the perspective of your body. What does it want you to know?

_____

_____

_____

_____

_____

_____

_____

_____

_____

_____

Breaking free from unhealthy and unattainable standards of beauty is one of the most empowering journeys in life. What has society taught you about how your body "should" look? What do *you* think is truly beautiful or attractive? Take the power of defining beauty back into your own hands, as you write a description of what "beauty" is to you. Return to this description anytime you need inspiration.

GENTLE TOUCH

Let's explore the art of giving and receiving with a simple self-massage you can do anytime.

1. Set aside 10 to 15 minutes alone to connect with your body.

2. Begin by gently touching your face with your fingertips. Notice what feels good for you. Do you prefer a lighter touch or something stronger? Adapt and respond to your own needs.

3. Continue by gently massaging your whole head, neck, and scalp. Notice any areas that need extra attention. Use a circular motion, firm pressure, or any other touch that feels good.

4. If you'd like, continue for the whole body.

Notice how good it feels to give and receive in your own body.

Feeling at home in our bodies starts with finding your resources. A *resource* is a healthy and uplifting experience you can go to in times of need. Resources might include places in nature, pets, mentors, good friends, spiritual connection, movement, art, or dancing. It can also be a thought, such as a blissful memory, remembering someone from your past, or an affirmation. What are your resources? Start an ongoing list here and refer to it when your body needs support.

_____

_____

_____

_____

_____

_____

_____

_____

_____

_____

Is there any part of your body that you judge? Begin to heal this judgmental pattern right now by writing down 5 things you appreciate about those parts of you. You might say, "My thighs are strong; they help me run and dance; they have beautiful curves; they feel warm and soft; they got me this far in life." Come back to this prompt whenever you notice self-judgment arising.

_____

_____

_____

_____

_____

_____

_____

_____

_____

_____

GROUNDING AND PRESENCE

Grounding practices help us stay comfortably present in our bodies. When we are present in our bodies, we can access intuition, awareness of our heart's desires, gut feelings, and emotional intelligence. Try the following grounding practices and then choose your favorite to practice on a regular basis.

- Walk barefoot on the earth.

- While standing, bend forward to touch your toes. Relax and imagine tension draining out your fingertips for 30 seconds.

- Turn the major joints in your body in circles, slowly and smoothly, starting with the ankles, then the knees, hips, elbows, shoulders, and neck.

- Imagine an invisible cord coming from the base of your spine and connecting you all the way to the center of the Earth. For 1 minute, let your worries fall down that cord.

- Spend 2 minutes being entirely mindful of your body. Feel your back resting, your feet on the floor, and your breath flowing in and out.

Think of the magic of the foot, comparatively small, upon which your whole weight rests. It's a miracle and the dance is a celebration of that miracle.

—MARTHA GRAHAM

Sometimes when opening ourselves to pleasure, we encounter blocks of unworthiness or fear of disappointment or losing control. Write a letter to yourself explaining why you're deserving of pleasure and why it's okay. Read it whenever you need a reminder of your right to experience pleasures fully.

Write about a pleasurable moment in your body. What were you doing? It can be anything from tasting delicious chocolate cake to an intimate sexual experience. Describe the feeling of pleasure in detail. What was it like? How did it feel? If any shame comes up, pause and remember that it's okay to feel pleasure.

_____

_____

_____

_____

_____

_____

_____

_____

_____

_____

_____

Sensuality helps us enjoy our bodies. When we connect to our bodies through sensuality, we feel energized and refreshed. What makes you feel "sensual"? Is it wearing soft clothing, feeling warm water in the shower, sifting your toes through the sand, or something else? How can you integrate more sensuality into your daily life?

_____

_____

_____

_____

_____

_____

_____

_____

_____

_____

_____

SLOW DOWN

Each day, we rush through experiences that could bring us great pleasure if we just slowed down. Let's discover new layers and nuances of our senses—smell, taste, sight, touch, and sound—by slowing down and being mindful and present to the experience. If you don't experience all five senses, work with the ones you do have.

1. Find an object you like for each of the five senses. For example: essential oils (smell), fruit or chocolate (taste), a beautiful flower (sight), a feather (touch), and a bell (sound).

2. Spend 1 full minute exploring each item, immersing yourself in the sensory experience. Breathe deeply and let yourself receive.

3. Notice the sensory pleasure of each item and how it makes you feel, physically and emotionally.

How can you experience simple pleasures in your life more often and fully?

Learning the language of your body will help you recognize its wisdom and understand what it is telling you. Let's practice describing sensations in your body. Choose any area. It could be something like "My belly feels soft, warm, open." Other descriptions might be hot, cold, tingly, heavy, charged, wavy, tight, etc. Visual insights might also emerge, for example, "My belly feels filled with golden honey." Practice the language of sensation as things happen throughout your day and record your insights here.

_____

_____

_____

_____

_____

_____

_____

_____

_____

Our intuitive body wisdom provides guidance, inspiration, clarity, and strength. Write your intuition or gut-sense feelings on any topic or situation in your life. Don't think about it too much—just let the words flow from a deeper place inside of you. Place your hand on your low belly to get in touch with your body's wisdom. Keep adding spontaneous insights here as they arise, and feel free to continue in a notebook once this space is filled.

_____

_____

_____

_____

_____

_____

_____

_____

_____

_____

NEW PLEASURES

The divine feminine helps us to be fully present in our lives. When we are busy doing tasks, we often miss things because we're not truly present to our experience. We can discover new, surprising pleasures by slowing down and paying attention.

1. Choose one activity you do nearly every day, such as washing dishes, making your bed, or brushing your teeth.

2. Instead of automatically performing this task, do it very slowly, paying close attention to your sensory experience. What do you see, smell, taste, hear, and feel? Can you find new pleasure in this experience?

3. Spend extra time with any pleasurable sensations, such as the warm water on your hands or the smell of fresh bedsheets. Reflect on how simple daily tasks can be experienced in a nourishing way.

Life can sometimes feel overwhelming. It's important to be aware of what is too much for you, in order to regulate your nervous system. Reflect on the past week or month—which moments were overwhelming for you? What could have supported you in those moments? Write about how you can prepare to have support ready when you need it next.

_____

_____

_____

_____

_____

_____

_____

_____

_____

Sexual energy is the most potent energy we carry in our bodies—it's the energy to create life! Being in touch with it can awaken power, wisdom, and healing within us. Describe your sexual energy. What is at the root of your desire? What fulfills your sexual energy? What makes it feel safe to come out? What awakens it? Write your thoughts on this and how you can protect and support this part of you.

_____

_____

_____

_____

_____

_____

_____

_____

_____

_____

EXPRESS, RELEASE, EMBODY

In this exercise, we'll practice moving an emotion through our bodies to express it, release it, or deeply embody it. Choose an emotion you have been feeling lately—it can be pleasant or unpleasant, but don't choose something too overwhelming. Perhaps try gratitude, nostalgia, sadness, passion, or joy.

1. Find a song that feels like a good match for your emotion.

2. Play it alone, so you can more easily move around free of self-consciousness.

3. Dance or make shapes that express this emotion. How does your feeling move? What is the shape of your emotion? Express yourself without holding back.

How do you feel after dancing? If you enjoyed this technique, use it anytime you want to move through an emotion.

Imagine your body as a sacred temple—a place to house and honor your soul. What would this temple look like, and of what materials is it made? Which offerings would you make in this temple? You can offer it anything—even love. What songs would you sing to honor this sacred space? Who, or what, can you imagine as temple guards? Notice what happens as you imagine your body as a temple and perform one small act to honor it.

_____

_____

_____

_____

_____

_____

_____

_____

_____

_____

_____

Practice appreciating yourself by writing a love letter to your body. What do you love about your body? Do you love how it dances? How it appreciates the taste of exotic foods? Do you love the shape of your toes or the feeling of your hair? Create a deeper bond with and appreciation for yourself by expressing gratitude for your body.

_____

_____

_____

_____

_____

_____

_____

_____

_____

_____

CELEBRATE YOUR BODY

Celebrating our bodies on a regular basis helps us to live full, happy, healthy lives. Honor your body with a simple ritual. Reflect on your gratitude from the previous prompt. Keep this in mind as you design your ritual.

Some ideas for inspiration are:

- Make a beautiful bath with flower petals, candles, and tea

- Hike into nature and express your gratitude aloud

- Light some incense and a candle and dance out your gratitude

- Make a healthy feast to share with others

- Pamper yourself with a massage or homemade facial treatment

This is a moment to celebrate your body. Enjoy it! Repeat this exercise on a regular basis, like your own "self-care Sunday."

My body is my
sacred home.

You can't use up
creativity. The more
you use, the more
you have.

—MAYA ANGELOU

SECTION 3

LET YOUR CREATIVITY FLOW

Ancient cultures worshipped the divine feminine through sacred water wells aligned with the moon and stars. Imagine if the divine feminine lived in a sacred well within you. How could you access this water within? One way is by connecting to your creative energy. Creativity naturally brings us to a sense of aliveness, awe, and wonder, aligning us with our spiritual center.

The journey to finding and expressing your creativity might bring you face to face with judgment, fear, and perfectionism—especially if you're not used to it. I encourage you to treat this section as a blank canvas. Let your brain work in new ways. Allow inspiration to move you. Surrender to the inner spring of creativity within you—it is divine.

This section will guide you into the creative energy that is uniquely yours. We'll explore ways to move past creative blocks and implement new ideas to get your juices flowing. The prompts and exercises in this section will help you carve a path for your divine feminine essence to flow.

Reflect on the role creativity has played throughout your life. Write the story of your creative energy, from childhood until now, as if it were a story about a friend. When did you meet? What did you like to do? Were you ever close? Did the friendship change or did you grow distant? If so, when and why? Share your story here.

_____

_____

_____

_____

_____

_____

_____

_____

_____

_____

What are you curious about? Write down all the subjects you'd love to learn about or experience. Let yourself dream—don't hold back for lack of time, money, or a sense of what's "realistic." Imagine you had all the time and money in the world to explore any area. Would you choose race car driving, French baking skills, indigenous plant wisdom, interior design, or something else? Keep adding to this list as new ideas come to you.

_____

_____

_____

_____

_____

_____

_____

_____

_____

_____

_____

CREATIVE ENERGY FLOW

What does your creative energy look like? Think back to a time when you felt creativity flowing through you. It might have been recent, or as far back as childhood. If you can't think of a time, simply imagine how it would feel. What were you doing? What did it feel like?

Immerse yourself in the details of that memory or image. Close your eyes, take a deep breath, and feel your body. What is the feeling of your creativity? Can you see any colors? How does the energy move inside you—outward, inward, quickly, slowly? Do you see any shapes, symbols, places, animals, words, or people? Let your answers come intuitively. Feel free to use the space below or a separate piece of paper to draw your own unique creative energy.

We all have times when our creative juices feel inaccessible. Feeling "blocked" creatively is where most of us begin! Think about a creative block you might have experienced. Write from the perspective of the block, as if it could speak. What does it want? How does it sound? How long has it been there, and what makes it come and go? As creative blocks arise, spend some time discovering what they are about.

_____

_____

_____

_____

_____

_____

_____

_____

_____

_____

One harmful event can sometimes block our creative potential. Look back to a time when your creativity wasn't honored, such as when someone ridiculed your work. Write about what happened. Can you reframe this experience in a way that provides closure and peace to you? If you can't think of a specific incident, write how you imagine your life with full creative expression. How would your life be different if you had unhindered access to your creativity?

_____

_____

_____

_____

_____

_____

_____

_____

_____

_____

_____

Many geniuses who walked this Earth had very peculiar methods for accessing their creativity. Albert Einstein took bubble baths and saw equations in dreams. Nikola Tesla walked for miles every day. Philosopher and mathematician Émilie du Châtelet was famous for her active sex life. What helps you access your creativity? If you can't think of anything, take some guesses as to what might work. Come up with a plan to try it out.

_____

_____

_____

_____

_____

_____

_____

_____

_____

SPARKING AWE AND WONDER

When was the last time you experienced feelings of awe or wonder? This energy opens up our sense of possibility, mystery, and magic in the world.

Tonight, step outside and spend 15 minutes looking at the night sky. If you can see stars, enjoy their beauty. If not, look for the moon or simply gaze upward. Think about anything that inspires you, such as all the amazing facts we know about nature, life, and the human experience. Reflect on what you have learned in your life. What has been awe-inspiring, beautiful, or meaningful? Take a "big picture" view and spark this magic within yourself.

Afterwards, write down any moments of wonder and inspiration in a notebook or journal. Revisit these words when you need a dose of awe in your life.

Imagine you were exploring outer space and found a distant planet that was a perfect utopia for you. What would that planet be like? What would it be named? Describe everything in detail, like the climate and terrain, any animals or other life-forms, and how daily life is lived. Let your creative juices flow to create your dream world. What does this planet reveal about who you are?

_____

_____

_____

_____

_____

_____

_____

_____

_____

_____

_____

The wild nature of divine feminine energy allows us to use our creativity in innovative ways. Play with this capacity by connecting two unrelated sensory experiences through metaphors. For example, I might describe tasting my favorite food as "like melting into a pink sunset," or hearing my favorite music as "tasting the salt of my lover's sweat." Choose a favorite smell, taste, sight, touch, and sound and describe it with your wild inspiration.

_____

_____

_____

_____

_____

_____

_____

_____

_____

_____

EMBRACE PLAY

Play is a lost art for adults, but it shouldn't be! Play helps rewire neuropathways, relaxes the nervous system, opens creativity, and brings spontaneous joy. It leads us to our divine feminine inner sanctuary.

Spend 5 minutes playing. Put on a song, dance, jump around, or do a somersault. Spin in circles or kick your legs in the air. Make a mess—"un-make" your bed, throw a deck of cards, or toss pillows in the air. Do this alone or with friends (the latter is much more fun!).

Notice any parts in you that have resistance. Try moving past it until you feel a sense of freedom or liberation. Afterwards, sit or lie down in silence for 2 to 5 minutes. Feel into your body. What do you feel? Can you connect to feelings of being alive and spontaneity?

Be wild; that is how to clear the river . . . If we want to allow it its freedom, we have to allow our ideational lives to be let loose, to stream, letting anything come, initially censoring nothing. That is creative life.

—DR. CLARISSA PINKOLA ESTÉS

The human body has been the source of artistic inspiration for millennia. Discover and honor the beauty of your body through poetic interpretation, describing body and sensations through metaphors. Some examples might be "Air blowing through my chest like a breezeway" or "mountainous landscape of luscious flesh." What poetic inspiration can you find from your body or inner experience? Write about how this makes you feel.

_____

_____

_____

_____

_____

_____

_____

_____

_____

_____

To tap into your spontaneous creativity, write a poem, song, or rhyme about the next 3 things you see. For example: chair, sunlight, cat. In the space provided, write a four-line verse (or longer if you like). Work freely with any silly inspiration that comes. My inspiration was: "I sat in the chair, my cat had no hair, the sunlight's glare made him bare, I dared not to stare." Have fun with it!

_____

_____

_____

_____

_____

_____

_____

_____

_____

_____

CREATIVE OFFERING

Choose one creative activity and do it as an offering to the divine feminine energy that lives inside of you, others, and all of life. Or, choose a quality to offer, such as compassion, beauty, or harmony. You can also make an energetic offering to specific people or communities. The idea is that the act is an offering of energy to something greater than yourself.

Some ideas to try: cooking, dancing, writing, painting, composing music, singing, scrapbooking, sewing, gardening, etc.

1. Connect with your gratitude and devotion before doing this activity with 1 minute of silence.

2. Internally state your intention that this act is an offering and that the rewards of pleasure or accolades be given to a higher purpose.

3. Let yourself be carried away by the energy of devotion.

When creativity is fed by devotion, magic happens.

Practical creativity—creativity with an agenda, like organizing a closet or problem-solving—can be enhanced by divine feminine energy. Consider an area you want to improve. List the issues and start brainstorming potential solutions. Can you find a new perspective? Spend 15 minutes contemplating this topic, with space for embodied movement or spacious silence. Feel into your body's intuition and write what springs from there. Try this anytime you feel stuck.

When we really look, we all have poignant experiences in our lives that are impactful and filled with wisdom. Describe at least one significant experience below that stands out in your life. Include the struggle or challenge and the lessons learned. What in your story could inspire or comfort others?

_____

_____

_____

_____

_____

_____

_____

_____

_____

_____

LET GO OF PERFECTION

Let's practice a drawing or painting exercise that can help free you from unnecessary standards of perfection. Gather your supplies and make space in your schedule to be creative. Use any materials you wish.

1. Pause briefly before starting to get centered.

2. As you move toward your paper or canvas, try drawing or painting with your nondominant hand. Trust that what will come through you will be right. You don't have to depict anything specific; just let your impulses take over. Let your hand become an extension of a deeper space inside your body. Keep going for a minute or two.

3. Switch to your dominant hand, finishing what you started in any creative way you wish.

4. Take a moment to appreciate your creation. Remember, there are no mistakes!

One place we forget to be creative is in our self-expression. We sometimes construct a personality that fits into the social structure around us, instead of from inner inspiration and authenticity. Who are you, deep down? Write your positive qualities that make you feel most like yourself. What are the most treasured parts of yourself that you want more of a chance to express? Reflect on your next opportunity to do this.

_____

_____

_____

_____

_____

_____

_____

_____

_____

_____

Imagine a conversation between your soul and your creativity. Visualize them in any form that makes intuitive sense (colors, light, beings, shapes, etc.) and see them turning toward each other and connecting. What might they say to each other? How connected are they? Is there anything that could make them closer? What could they create together? Help your creativity flow from a deeper place by imagining this conversation, and write about the details and your insights.

_____

_____

_____

_____

_____

_____

_____

_____

_____

_____

DANCE!

Dance is an especially sacred form of expression because it's intimately connected to the movement of your soul. When you let your body be the canvas upon which inspiration paints its colors, you'll find that your divine feminine energy awakens.

1. Reflect on a meaningful or joyful experience in your life. For example, an inner spiritual experience, having a child, falling in love, or swimming with dolphins.

2. Make a 10-minute playlist of music that reflects your experience.

3. Create a dance or spontaneous movement as an offering to that experience. Tell the story through your body. Let go of self-consciousness and let the music take you deeper. Surrender to your emotions. Let your body move any way it wants. Just keep moving and returning to movement that feels good to you.

Notice how you feel afterwards. Did you express something meaningful through your body?

Researchers have found 8 different categories of how creativity is expressed: interpersonal (with others), intrapersonal (within yourself), verbal-language, logical-mathematical, visual, bodily (kinesthetic), musical, and naturalistic (environmental awareness). List these in order of what resonates with you, from most to least. How can you enhance or nurture your top three creative preferences?

_____

_____

_____

_____

_____

_____

_____

_____

_____

_____

What if your creative self had full permission to express itself in all ways? What directions would your inspiration take you? What would be your next step? Describe your fully expressed life. Which things can you start doing this week? Write down an action plan and set time in your calendar for your next creative experience. Then reflect on it in the space below.

_____

_____

_____

_____

_____

_____

_____

_____

_____

_____

_____

TAKE A LEAP

Accessing our creativity is a big leap for many. The next step is to share it. When we expose our creative work, we expose parts of our soul, and that can be scary. The reward isn't in the accolades, but in having a witness to your sacred creativity.

Take something you've created from this book or somewhere else in your life and share it with another human. You can also create something as a gift for another. Notice how it feels to share yourself. What's it like to let this part of your soul unfold into the world? If you don't feel that you have a safe person to share with, intend to find someone soon and keep your eyes and heart open.

The source of my creativity is infinite. It makes me feel alive.

[The Earth] is mother of all that is natural, mother of all that is human. She is mother of all, for contained in her are the seeds of all.

—ST. HILDEGARD VON BINGEN

NURTURE YOUR RELATIONSHIP WITH MOTHER EARTH

The sun on your face, the wind passing by, the silence of the forest—these are raw, visceral experiences of the divine feminine. When we go into nature, our hearts can have direct encounter and communication with Mother Earth. Our souls sense this intuitively and are effortlessly restored with as little as a walk through a silent forest.

Our intimate connections with nature keep us grounded in reality, allowing us to find the essence of spirituality here on Earth, rather than in an imaginary or hypothetical place in our minds.

Many of the exercises in this book are action-based to support your journey of becoming a steward of the planet—we're no longer in an era where we can ignore the urgent needs of the environment. In this section, you'll find insightful prompts to deepen your connection with nature, and get inspired to use your power to take action.

How connected do you feel to nature? Life can be so full and busy that we easily overlook this relationship, but even simply taking in the beauty of a tree or grassy area near your workplace can reconnect you. How can you connect with nature more? Write some ideas, then follow through on one or more. Any step toward nature brings you closer to the heart of the divine feminine.

_____

_____

_____

_____

_____

_____

_____

_____

_____

_____

What was the very first place in nature that you remember connecting to? How old were you? Think back on your childhood, a time when life was much more vivid and nature could be deeply impactful. What memories do you have of being outside as a kid? Describe your favorite places in nature and what you loved about them.

_____

_____

_____

_____

_____

_____

_____

_____

_____

NATURAL BEAUTY

Reacquaint yourself with the beauty of nature by creating a found-object mandala. A mandala is a circular design with repeating patterns around a center motif, representing the layers of the self. The center symbolizes one's inner sanctum, where the soul or home of your divine feminine energy resides.

Create a nature mandala to represent the divine feminine inside of you. Refer to the Resources on page 158 for inspiration. Spend 15 to 20 minutes outside gathering leaves, rocks, sticks, flowers, grass—anything you can find. The more you collect, the bigger and more elaborate your mandala can be. Design your mandala on a flat surface, starting with the center object. What will you place to represent your spiritual center? Enjoy the process and beauty of this piece of nature. Afterwards, you can share your mandala with others if you choose!

Which part of nature best reflects your soul? Take a moment to envision a landscape that represents your spiritual center. Close your eyes, place your hand on your heart or belly, and let an image come to you spontaneously. You might see a majestic, silent, and vast desert; a vibrant, verdant jungle; a spring-fed waterfall. What does this image mean to you? Write about your connection to this particular landscape.

_____

_____

_____

_____

_____

_____

_____

_____

_____

_____

The elements of nature are access points of the divine feminine. What experiences have you had connecting with them? Describe meaningful moments you've had with the earth (gardens, landscapes), water (oceans, rivers, lakes), fire (bonfires, hot days, volcanoes), air (windy places, looking at the clouds, breath), and space (starry nights). If you can't think of anything, refer to the next exercise to begin your journey connecting with the elements.

CONNECTING WITH THE ELEMENTS

Spend at least 5 minutes in a natural outdoor setting without distractions. Any outdoor space will work. If you're in a city, you may need to find a park for this exercise, ideally with a fountain, stream, or pond. Bring a bottle of clean, pure water with you.

Spend a full minute immersing into each element. Bring your curiosity and mindfulness as you explore, noticing your sensory experience of each element. What is it like to experience the elements more deeply?

Earth: Notice colors and textures; touch the dirt; smell the soil; walk barefoot.

Water: Let water run through your fingers; drink from your water bottle; gaze at the water; listen to water flowing; watch the patterns.

Fire: Feel the warmth of the sun; observe its shadows; marvel at its power; soak up the heat.

Air: Feel the breeze or air quality; look at the sky or clouds; watch birds, trees, and leaves gently moving.

Space: Take in all the other elements at once.

The land you live on has witnessed more than any single human life. Write from the perspective of the land where you currently reside. What events were witnessed by this land? What groups of people have lived there? You don't have to be historically accurate—the point is to explore the perspective of the Earth and discern its wisdom. What advice or wisdom might the Earth give to humans from its perspective?

_____

_____

_____

_____

_____

_____

_____

_____

_____

_____

Just as we have human needs, the Earth also has needs. What do you imagine are her needs? To have her beauty perceived by her creatures? To have uninterrupted ecosystems, clean rivers, safe homes for animals? To have her longevity considered like we consider our own? Take a moment to listen. Write down the needs of the Earth. What big or small ways can you help fulfill those needs?

_____

_____

_____

_____

_____

_____

_____

_____

_____

_____

MINDFUL EATING

Food is like our umbilical cord to Mother Earth. When we eat from her bounty, we notice well-being in our body, mind, and spirit.

This following exercise is meant to support your journey of reconnecting to nature. Proceed gently and lovingly, with openness and curiosity. If you notice any self-judgment or shame arising, feel free to stop.

1. Think about the food you eat: Is most of it canned, packaged, or wrapped in plastic? Or is it fresh and straight from the Earth?

2. Try eating more in line with nature for one full day. Eat meals outside, take a moment for gratitude before each meal, introduce organic veggies, or try vegetarian or vegan cuisine.

3. Notice how it feels to eat this way.

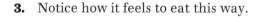

Feel free to expand this practice for a longer time, as you are inspired.

Looking around, we can see the incredible creativity of life—an endless expression of plants, flowers, landscapes, animals, insects, ocean creatures, humans—the list goes on. Think of the natural places, creatures, or experiences that have touched your heart. What moments in nature took your breath away? Write a letter of gratitude to Mother Earth for her beauty and creativity.

_____

_____

_____

_____

_____

_____

_____

_____

_____

_____

No man is as wise
as Mother Earth. She
has witnessed every
human day, every human
struggle, every human
pain, and every
human joy.

—ANASAZI FOUNDATION

For many spiritual traditions, the Earth is considered the literal body of the goddess: its rivers are her blood, its forests are her bones, its soil is her flesh. Close your eyes and imagine for a moment that this is true. How would it change or influence your life to experience the Earth in this way? How would you walk in nature or live on this planet differently?

_____

_____

_____

_____

_____

_____

_____

_____

_____

_____

A GLOBAL PERSPECTIVE

Divine feminine energy reveals the interconnectedness of life. As we embrace this energy inside ourselves, we naturally start to think more globally. Embracing a global perspective can enrich your life because you'll feel more connected as you care about something greater. You'll discover your place, purpose, and power amidst the "whole."

1. Choose an environmental issue you feel passionately about; it could be ocean pollution, forest degradation, animal extinction, protecting Indigenous lands, or recycling.

2. Find a reputable organization that works on this issue.

3. Join its newsletter, learn the associated social and political needs, or spread awareness as you are able. Donate time or money, if possible. Stay updated and let this awareness become integrated into your life.

4. Observe how your daily life choices can support change on this issue.

We all are descended from ancestors who had a spiritual relationship with nature. What kinds of spiritual beliefs did your ancestors have about the Earth? Go as far back as you need to. What rituals or spiritual practices did they perform? If you are not sure about your ancestry, you can write about any culture you feel drawn to. How can you respect their tradition? Can you integrate their wisdom into your life?

_____

_____

_____

_____

_____

_____

_____

_____

_____

_____

Nature is full of wisdom. There are many examples of mystics, shamans, and saints having spontaneous spiritual realizations in nature. And we can, too—a flowing river can inspire us to let go of thoughts, worries, and false identities, in order to find renewal. Write your intuitive sense of the wisdom inherent in waterfalls, rivers, lakes, oceans, mountains, jungles, fields, or deserts. What can they teach us? How can you integrate this into your life?

_____

_____

_____

_____

_____

_____

_____

_____

_____

_____

CONNECT WITH YOUR ENVIRONMENT

We have great power and influence over our local environment. What are the nearest natural places to your home? Consider any state parks, rivers, lakes, ponds, forests, deserts, or oceans. Who is stewarding or caring for these places? What kind of help might they need?

Take some time to connect with your local natural environments. You could make a plan to visit one of these places, connect with a local environmental or Indigenous organization, pick up trash on your next visit, donate to a preservation fund, or support initiatives to protect them.

As Nobel Prize–winning activist Wangari Maathai said: "It's the little things that citizens do. That's what will make the difference." Let her words inspire you on your journey.

The seasons of nature teach us about the natural cycles of growth, blossoming, decay, death, and renewal. In your own life, which phase do you feel you are currently in? You might have different phases for various parts of your life. For example, your career might be in a blossoming phase, while your spirituality is in a renewal phase. Reflect and write about them, including what the next phases might look like for you.

Immersing ourselves in nature gives us direct contact with the divine feminine. If we do this with awareness of how it affects us, we can open doors to healing and inspiration. What does nature touch inside of you? What is it like to be absorbed with nature's beauty? What does it feel like? Think back to moments of deep immersion into nature. Memorialize your internal experiences here.

NATURE MEDITATION

Set aside 20 minutes for a nature meditation. This is a wonderful exercise to do with a friend.

1. Sit comfortably on the ground, ideally keeping the spine straight. Feel free to bring a chair or blanket to sit on.

2. Visualize a cord extending from your perineum or the soles of your feet down into the center of the Earth.

3. Imagine the Earth is recharging your body's battery—your energy and vitality—through this cord. Let each breath soften your tensions and connect you to Earth's vital energy.

4. Notice your body gradually relaxing. Once you're deeply relaxed, visualize a cord rising from the top of your head up into the cosmos, bringing fresh cosmic energy to revitalize you.

5. Spend as much time as you'd like feeling into these connections.

We often have a wild side, about which we might feel ashamed or judged. Reclaim your wild side by imagining it as a force of nature. For example, "Sometimes a volcano of energy bursts in me" or "I get lightning strikes of spontaneous ideas." What can inspire you to explore your wild side more? How will you do it? Write about it in the space below.

We often say the Earth is your mother, but she is also your lover. Express this love by writing a passionate love letter to the Earth as if she were your beloved. You can use juicy, enticing metaphors, such as "Your kisses are like dandelions wet with morning dew; the wind of your breath makes my body come alive." Have fun with it! In what ways can you fall in love with the Earth?

Even though we can sometimes feel discouraged about our Earth's problems, it's vital to envision the potential planet we can have and never give up—every choice makes a difference. What kind of a planet would you like to pass to future generations? What kinds of changes do you want to see? Write about your vision of the Earth. Keep it close to your heart and let it influence your choices.

_____

_____

_____

_____

_____

_____

_____

_____

_____

_____

VOW TO MOTHER EARTH

A vow made in nature is sacred. Let's make a sacred vow to Mother Earth. You can promise to honor and protect her, commit to make ecofriendly choices, or be a witness to her sacred beauty, for example.

1. Write a vow in your own words.

2. Find a quiet spot in nature. Bring a blanket and some offerings—flowers, water, special stones. Try not to bring anything an animal could get sick from or that is disruptive to the ecosystem. (Make sure to take home what you brought with you, as well.)

3. Sit quietly for 10 minutes, listening to the sounds of nature.

4. Reflect on your gratitude and devotion for nature as you place offerings directly on the earth.

5. State your vow aloud, with Mother Earth as your witness.

I connect with my
soul through nature
and honor Mother
Earth with my actions.

We have all known
the long loneliness and
we have learned that
the only solution is love
and that love comes
with community.

—DOROTHY DAY

DRAW WISDOM AND STRENGTH FROM YOUR COMMUNITY

At the heart of divine feminine energy is connection—connection to the self, the planet, to spirit or the divine, and to others. One of the most valuable parts of life is our relationships. Through our relationships, we know who we are and find purpose. The right people or community can nourish us more than any wellness program, diet, or exercise. True friendship brings satisfaction beyond any amount of success or money. Scientists are continuously discovering the power of a strong support network, especially for recovery and mental health. In short, we need each other.

However, for many today, meaningful relationships and community are sorely lacking. Social media can offer some sense of connection, but a thousand likes on a post cannot compare to true connection with friends or someone you love. In this section, you'll be guided to build supportive community, remember the value of true friendship, set boundaries, and get inspired to serve those around you.

In special moments of connection, we find our souls deeply nourished. What are some favorite memories that you have of others? Think of carefree fun times, meaningful conversations, or moments when you felt supported and understood. Who are the special people who have touched your life?

_____

_____

_____

_____

_____

_____

_____

_____

_____

_____

Who you spend time with greatly affects what your life is like. Who is in your close community? Think about 5 people you talk to or interact with on a regular basis. Write their names below and describe your relationships with each. How do they nourish you? Write down their admirable qualities and how they support you. If you find naming any close relationships to be a challenge, refer to the next exercise for support.

_____

_____

_____

_____

_____

_____

_____

_____

SOCIAL MAP

In the space below, use a pencil and write in the center circle, your name plus 2 to 5 names of those closest to you. In the larger circle, write up to 12 additional names of people whom you consider close and interact with often. Finally, outside the circles, write names of people or groups you interact with more casually.

Look over your map. When you see yourself in the center, do you feel supported? Does anyone drain your energy? If so, think about how you can shift things around, or perhaps add more supportive people into your social circles. Keep adjusting until your map feels right to you.

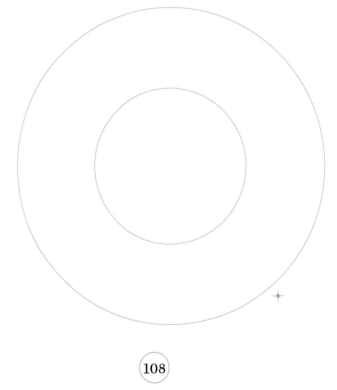

When we don't speak our truth, we often feel discomfort. I remember all the times in my life I didn't speak up—it hurts! Write down a time when you held back from speaking your truth and write what you *wanted* to say. Afterwards, place your hand on your heart and have compassion for yourself in those moments. Part of healing is self-forgiveness. How can you speak your truth next time?

_____

_____

_____

_____

_____

_____

_____

_____

_____

Our unseen or spiritual community is a part of our life. Who is a part of your unseen community? In the space below, write about your ancestors or loved ones who have passed on, as well as any spiritual guides or divine forms you feel connected to. How are they supporting or connected to you? After writing, take a moment to remember and reflect on them with love.

_____

_____

_____

_____

_____

_____

_____

_____

_____

_____

WEB OF CONNECTION

The divine feminine can be symbolized by a web of interconnectedness. The following meditation will help you connect to others you love.

1. Set aside 15 minutes of quiet time.

2. Sit comfortably with your back straight.

3. Feel your body resting and your heart rate slowing down.

4. Close your eyes and imagine an invisible thread emanating from your heart's center. Let this thread expand outward and connect to the heart of someone you love. Feel your hearts connect.

5. Let the thread weave into the heart of someone else you love, whether living or passed on. Allow it to weave without breaking, through the heart of as many people as you'd like, from your past, present, or future. See and feel this beautiful web.

6. Close with a thought of gratitude and let the web dissolve, knowing it's always with you.

Who's in your "heart community"? Your heart community is a group of people who share your values, uplift you, and give you strength. As we grow and evolve, we sometimes weave in and out of groups. Write about any groups that come to mind, past or present. If you haven't found your heart community yet, write down the values you'd like them to possess. How can your heart community strengthen and support you?

_____

_____

_____

_____

_____

_____

_____

_____

_____

_____

Embracing the divine feminine can heal our wounds of envy and competition. List people you envy or feel competitive with. Write what inspires you about that person. If it's a quality you can also develop, make a commitment to grow in that quality. If it's something that's uniquely theirs, let it be theirs. Come back and ask yourself, "What are my good qualities?" Nurture yourself by remembering and honoring the good in you.

_____

_____

_____

_____

_____

_____

_____

_____

_____

_____

A NEW PERSPECTIVE

When we step out of our perspective and see things from a bigger point of view, we can find deeper meaning, wisdom, and value in our choices. This exercise gives you a chance to practice this.

1. Choose a current issue, choice, or dilemma in your life.

2. Make three overlapping circles on the ground, one bigger than the other. This can be done with a small, medium, and large towel or blanket, with one on top of the other. The center circle represents your personal view of the issue. The second layer is your community, family, or affected group's view. The outermost layer represents the global perspective.

3. As you stand on each layer, reflect on the issue from that point of view.

4. Consider what new insights you've discovered, how your feelings change with new perspectives, and how this exercise influences your choices.

Compassion for ourselves and others inspires us to serve the greater community. Who or what groups might feel excluded or marginalized in your community? Have you ever felt excluded? Write your thoughts from a place of compassion for yourself or others who may feel this way. What kind of support can be given to people feeling excluded or marginalized?

_____

_____

_____

_____

_____

_____

_____

_____

_____

_____

_____

When we choose to love, we choose to move against fear, against alienation and separation. The choice to love is a choice to connect, to find ourselves in the other.

—BELL HOOKS

Each of us is born into an environment that affects who we are. Some examples could be expectations regarding body image, racial prejudice, gender beliefs, or environmental degradation. What challenging contexts may have conditioned or affected you? Write down the changes you wish to see in the world. What small step can you take today to help create a better world in this way?

_____

_____

_____

_____

_____

_____

_____

_____

_____

_____

SUPPORT YOUR COMMUNITY

As individuals, we have the power to support others on a local and global scale. Let your heart guide you in this two-part exercise.

Part 1: What are your local community's needs? How can you give back? Take at least one step in serving your local community. Some ideas could be ordering a subscription to your local paper, donating food, or volunteering.

Part 2: Until all humans can live with safe, affordable access to food, water, shelter, and health care, we have urgent work to do on this planet. Which societies outside of your own can you support? Choose a group outside of your local community and find a way you can offer support, even if it's simply staying informed. You might be inspired to learn about farmers' struggles in India or donate to groups ending child sex trafficking.

How does it feel to connect to your local and global communities?

Divine feminine wisdom dispels the myths of superiority and inferiority. No human is better or worse than another. How have you been affected by ideas of superiority and inferiority at work or school or with political, religious, or social groups? Reimagine those moments with a sense of equality. Take time to reflect and write about how things could be different. What role can you play in fostering change?

_____

_____

_____

_____

_____

_____

_____

_____

_____

For a tree to grow and bear fruit, it must connect to its roots. As humans, our roots are the people who raised us and our genetic inheritance. Honor your roots by writing a letter to your parents, guardians, foster family, or other caretakers or mentors. What can you thank them for? If you cannot find reasons to thank them, simply write: "I am grateful for my life" and consider what parts you are grateful for.

_____

_____

_____

_____

_____

_____

_____

_____

_____

_____

APPRECIATIVE ACTS

Reflect on someone in your life you appreciate. Do you have a great friend who makes you feel loved and seen? Do you feel gratitude for someone in your family? Are you inspired by a coach, teacher, or mentor? By not taking our relationships for granted, we can appreciate the valuable connections we have around us.

Today, show your appreciation for these people in a small, but meaningful way. Some ideas to get started might be calling to tell them how much you love them, making a card or writing a letter of gratitude, baking cookies, or sending a gift basket.

Enjoy the fruits of sharing your love and appreciation. Repeat this exercise as often as desired.

Who has shown up for you in your life, and how have you received their support? List the people, organizations, or structures that helped you in times of need. Even if they don't get it right all the time, it can still count for the effort and care they put forth. What does your support network look like? What can you do to appreciate them more?

_____

_____

_____

_____

_____

_____

_____

_____

_____

What would be an ideal community experience for you? The aim is to discover what your heart desires, so let your imagination run wild, without holding back. You could write about gathering on the cliffs of the ocean to watch the sunset, an intimate heart-opening dinner, cocreating an artistic project or business, or dancing in a flash mob. What do you long for? Write about how you can make it happen someday.

_____

_____

_____

_____

_____

_____

_____

_____

_____

GENUINE LOVE

The flow of genuine love can be the strongest medicine in times of need. In this exercise, we'll send loving thoughts toward those who are suffering.

1. Set aside 10 minutes when you can be undisturbed.

2. Sit comfortably and rest into stillness. For 1 minute, place your hand on your heart or belly. Feel nurtured with each breath, growing in compassion and love.

3. Visualize someone from your close circle who is struggling. Send loving energy to them, and feel them in your heart. Bathe them with golden light, visualize their healing, imagine solutions to their issues, or ask the divine to support them—whatever method works best for you.

4. Repeat for your larger community (coworkers, acquaintances, etc.) and then for the entire planet (specific groups struggling right now).

How can you shine in your community? What qualities or skills do you have to offer? Let yourself brag a little bit here; don't hold back. You may have a skill set like giving advice, making the best tacos, or knowing great hiking spots. Also, consider skills like empathy, compassion, joyfulness, and being kind to strangers. Write down your gifts and appreciate who you are. Make a plan to share more of your skills with someone you trust.

_____

_____

_____

_____

_____

_____

_____

_____

_____

_____

Who or what do you consider your family? "Family" is for you to define. You might consider your best friends, your pets, or plants as part of your family. Or your family might be your kids and your partner. Who are your loved ones? Describe your family below. What are your favorite ways of spending time with your family?

_____

_____

_____

_____

_____

_____

_____

_____

_____

_____

When the inspiration to serve another comes to our hearts, it makes even mundane tasks fulfilling. When was the last time you felt the spirit of service? Who in your life shows good examples of this spirit? What makes you want to be of service? How do you want to serve others? Reflect on and write about this inspiration in you.

_____

_____

_____

_____

_____

_____

_____

_____

_____

_____

GROWING COMMUNITY

Oftentimes, we want to build our community but don't know where to start.

Mark the date exactly 6 months from today on your calendar or record it in the space below. By now, you know much more about your values, interests, and what you can give to your community. Make an action plan of 5 steps you can take in the next 6 months to build your community network.

An example action plan might be:

1. Join a local chess club.

2. Reach out to a friend every week just to catch up.

3. Plan a costume-themed potluck dinner with friends.

4. Volunteer at the homeless shelter once a month.

5. Take a free yoga class at the park.

Mark the date here: _____.

Check back in 6 months. How has your community grown?

I love my
community. Through
community, I am nourished
and expanded.

When I dare to be
powerful, to use my
strength in the service
of my vision, then it
becomes less and less
important whether
I am afraid.

–AUDRE LORDE

SECTION 6

STEP INTO YOUR POWER

Divine feminine power is power *with* others, not power *over* others. We have become accustomed to seeing power as dangerous—something used against others, to hold people down and to cause harm. This is distorted power, not real power. Real power is integrated with divine feminine energy and comes from wholeness and presence. Real power is grounded in love. It can crack open a hardened soul to its tender core or inspire others to discover a new and better way of life.

We experience this power when we take actions inspired from the heart. The heart gives us the power to choose, create, protect, let go, and use our voices. Through our power, we can heal, share joy, love, and be vulnerable.

Using what you've learned so far, you'll practice stepping into your divine feminine power through prompts and exercises that ignite your fire. Let's get into it!

Divine feminine power gives us confidence, clarity, wisdom, and the capacity to take action. What makes you feel powerful? You might feel empowered waking up early, sharing your truth, or exercising—anything that gives you a feeling of strength. Reflect on a habit or experience that empowers you. How can you make those moments happen more often?

_____

_____

_____

_____

_____

_____

_____

_____

_____

_____

Images can inspire power within us because they have an impact on our subconscious. What is your power symbol? Close your eyes, open your imagination, and let it come to you. It could be an animal, such as a tiger, or an aspect of nature, such as a volcano or waterfall. You might see a color, a shape, or an image of yourself dancing, for example. Write about this power symbol. What does it mean to you?

_____

_____

_____

_____

_____

_____

_____

_____

_____

_____

POWER PRACTICE

The feeling of power must be practiced to make it a habit. This exercise will support and motivate you to practice embodying your power. Who or what inspires you to be powerful? Find a quote, image, or symbol that inspires your power. Refer to the last journal prompt for ideas, too. Print or draw it, and hang it in a place you will see every day.

Each morning when you first see it, stop what you are doing and pause for 10 seconds. Take a deep breath and connect to your body, feeling the sense of power as you remember what this quote, image, or symbol means to you. Familiarize yourself with this feeling of power and take it with you throughout your day.

Sometimes we are afraid to show or embody our power. This can be for many reasons. We might have seen someone abuse their power in the past. Do you believe it is okay for you to be powerful? What are you afraid might happen if you step forward with your full power in life? Express your fear on paper, then write a response to your fears, speaking sense to them from a place of compassion, love, and wisdom.

Was there a time in your life where you felt most empowered? Reflect on your life and write about that time. Maybe you were starting a new career path, pregnant with your first child, or training for an athletic competition. What can you learn from past moments of empowerment? What advice or insight would that version of yourself give you today?

IGNITE YOUR POWER CENTER

The Indian yogic spiritual tradition affirms that our power center is located in the torso, usually near the belly button. This exercise can be performed to ignite your power center, giving you confidence, dynamism, and willpower. Try it by yourself in the mornings to start your day.

1. Stand with your feet a little wider than shoulder-distance apart, toes facing forward.

2. Clasp your hands together as if you are holding an invisible sword.

3. Lift your clasped hands high above your head.

4. Take a step forward, and simultaneously bring your invisible sword down with the word, "HA!" Say it loudly and move with your full power.

5. Repeat as many times as you like within 1 minute.

Consider how you feel afterwards. Do you feel more powerful?

True power is like love—nothing is lost when given to another; it only expands for both. Who in your life has empowered you? You might have had a teacher, mentor, relative, or friend who encouraged you and built up your sense of capacity and power. How can you pass this empowerment forward to others?

_____

_____

_____

_____

_____

_____

_____

_____

_____

Society influences us to believe that sensitive qualities make us weak when, in fact, they give us a very deep power. What are your sensitive qualities? How do they empower you? For example, you might be empathetic and have a tender heart. This could give you the capacity to deeply understand people and lead from a place of love. What are the gifts of your sensitive qualities? How can you feel more empowered by them?

SETTING BOUNDARIES

Expressing clear boundaries is a foundation of empowerment. In this exercise, we'll practice saying *yes* and *no*, allowing you to practice using these words in a real-life moment.

1. Set aside 15 minutes alone or with a friend.

2. While standing, close your eyes and imagine someone asking a question that you want to say *no* to. An example could be: "Do you want to work late and finish all my reports for me?"

3. Give yourself full permission as you say *no* aloud in response. Notice what you feel in your body. Practice saying *no* at least 10 times as you imagine different questions.

4. Afterwards, do the same process for *yes*. An example could be: "Do you want to get ice cream?" Get comfortable feeling power in your body as you speak your truth.

The spark of divine feminine power is love—the kind of love that makes miracles happen. How powerful is your love? Write about times in your life when love moved you to act, reach out, or make a transformation. How can your love be transformative and impact the world in powerful ways? What other ways have you witnessed the power of love in people? Reflect on these questions and write about your experiences.

Don't forget love; it will bring all the madness you need to unfurl yourself across the universe.

—MIRABAI (MYSTIC POET; C. 1498–1546)

When we embrace divine feminine energy, we can discover the power to change our lives. Transformation takes a big surge of trust and energy as we're moving into the unknown. Have you ever been through a deep process of transformation? What was it like? Looking back on those moments, what words of encouragement or advice would you give yourself?

_____

_____

_____

_____

_____

_____

_____

_____

_____

_____

BIG CAT ENERGY

Humans have always looked to the animal kingdom to inspire power. Specifically, big cats such as lions, leopards, and tigers are common inspirations for power. By expressing big cat energy in our bodies, we can deepen our embodied power.

1. Set aside 10 minutes alone or with a friend.

2. Start by getting on your hands and knees. If this is uncomfortable or not possible, simply do the exercise standing or any way that feels comfortable for you.

3. Move around your room imagining yourself to be the big cat or animal of your choice. Enjoy your power! Go ahead and roar.

4. As you look around your space, how does it feel to be the king or queen of this jungle? What do you notice in your body?

Self-expression is powerful because it can deeply move, change, and impact others as well as the world around you. What types of expression make you feel the most powerful? Examples might be speaking, making music, dancing, writing, giving— How does it feel to experiment with your power as you express yourself? Write about your experiences in the space provided.

_____

_____

_____

_____

_____

_____

_____

_____

_____

_____

Music is an incredible and reliable way to ignite our power. What is your power song—something that fills you with enthusiasm, hope, and joy? Take a moment and scroll through your playlists to find a song that gives you power. What makes you light up with energy, strength, and determination? Why is this song empowering for you? Continue adding to your ongoing list of empowering songs here.

_____

_____

_____

_____

_____

_____

_____

_____

_____

POWERFUL GROWTH

Complaining and blaming is a drain on our power. Why? Because true power stands on a foundation of personal responsibility. When we complain or blame, we give our power away.

Make a commitment not to blame or complain for a set amount of time. It can be for one afternoon, one day, one week, or one month, depending on what you feel will challenge you. Choose an amount of time you know is realistically achievable—it's better to choose less time and be successful to build your confidence.

What changes inside of you as you practice this? Do you notice your quality of life is different? Consider what you will do with the growing power within you.

The capacity of surrender is a power of the divine feminine. We all have things in our lives that we cling to and refuse to let go of. What can you let go of? Maybe it's the outcome of a project or being liked by a certain person. What are you afraid of? Face your fears as you write them down. How does the ability to surrender strengthen your divine feminine power?

_____

_____

_____

_____

_____

_____

_____

_____

_____

_____

Many people feel disempowered in their sexuality because of past traumas or the weight of judgment, shame, or repression. Write a healing and inspiring letter to your sexuality to soothe your insecurities. You could start with: "To my sexuality, I know you have felt shame, and I want to assure you that it's okay to be you . . . " What words does your sexual energy long to hear? (See page 158 for additional resources.)

_____

_____

_____

_____

_____

_____

_____

_____

_____

_____

When exploring power in a practical way, we should also look at money. We live in a world where having our own money helps empower us. For example, sometimes people are afraid to leave an unhealthy relationship on which they are also financially dependent. How is your relationship with money? Is this an area where you can grow? Make an inspiring financial plan for yourself in the space provided. (See page 158 for additional resources.)

_____

_____

_____

_____

_____

_____

_____

_____

CELEBRATION RITUAL

Celebration is a pathway to power. When we celebrate cycles of completion or fruition, we honor ourselves for our work and achievements. This ritual strengthens our capacity to keep going. Too often, we forget to pause and celebrate who we are. Celebrating can be a fun, playful way to empower ourselves.

Create a celebration ritual. Reflect on your life right now, looking at your good qualities, your transformations, your community, your achievements. What have you not yet celebrated? What about a past milestone that was never properly recognized? Honor yourself in a creative way. You can bake a cake, have a solo dance party, or take a nice bath. Make your intention clear—this is a ritual to celebrate you! Notice the power that comes with recognizing this milestone. Enjoy!

The divine feminine empowers us to nurture inner harmony. Our power skyrockets when what we feel, say, and do are in alignment. Where in your life can you better express the feelings of your heart? Which feelings would you like to act on? What have you been saying you want, but not moving toward? Reflect and write about how you can be more aligned in thoughts, words, and actions.

_____

_____

_____

_____

_____

_____

_____

_____

_____

_____

Divine feminine power is limitless. It can nurture your most tender, vulnerable parts, and it can help you rise to your most desired heights. How would your life be different if you stepped fully into that power? Imagine you had the power to create *exactly* the life and relationships you want. What would it look like? How can you move toward this power?

_____

_____

_____

_____

_____

_____

_____

_____

_____

_____

YOUR AWAKENING

You've done so much hard work to get here—congrats! Take a moment to flip through and reflect on what you've experienced through this book.

What have you discovered about yourself? What new version of yourself wants to step forward? Record your insights and transformative experiences below. How is the divine feminine awakening in you? What has been your biggest lesson? Your biggest inspiration? The newest experience? Which new practices or habits do you want to cultivate in your everyday life? Write down what feels important to you.

My power comes
from an endless source
within me.

A FINAL WORD

We've come to the end of this phase of your divine feminine journey. It has been an absolute pleasure to walk this path with you.

Throughout this book, we've explored your unique divine feminine energy, tapped into deeper layers of pleasure in your body, and flowed with your creativity. We nurtured a connection to Mother Earth, built a supportive community, and embodied your power. I encourage you to keep resting back into your heart, listening to yourself, and trusting your intuition. Seek moments of beauty and connection with others. All of these will integrate the divine feminine into your body, mind, and daily life.

Divine feminine spirituality teaches us about *immanence*—the capacity to experience the divine directly through the world around us. That is the essential teaching of this book. The next time you're doing the dishes or tasting a piece of fruit, remember what you've learned about pleasure. As you hear about crises on the other side of the world, feel your connection as one human family. During your next experience in nature, aim to connect with Mother Earth. Gradually, these small experiences will expand and become more sustained, building a way of life.

You might return to this journal in a year and find your answers are completely different. This is the nature of the feminine inside of us—always changing, evolving, and expressing new creativity. Divine feminine energy can endlessly deepen. Each section was just an introduction to what could be a lifetime of deepening. I encourage you to continue exploring any area that stood out for you and seek instructors or teachings that support your journey. As you do, trust your inner guidance to lead the way.

May this journal touch hearts, nourish lives, and encourage positive change in the world.

RESOURCES

TO DEEPEN YOUR DIVINE FEMININE JOURNEY

Alisha J. Flecky (my website): AlishaFlecky.com
Discover, embody, and nurture your divine feminine energy with in-person international retreats, workshops, online groups, and somatic coaching.

Monika Nataraj: MonikaNataraj.net
In-person retreats and trainings diving into your divine feminine through mystical dance, meditation, tantric practices for women, and ritual.

Schirin Chams Diba: SchirinChamsDiba.com
Sacred folk dance, medicine, and mystical arts with Schirin Chams Diba.

Shakti Temple Arts: ShaktiTempleArts.com
A school of embodied feminine awakening through living tantra and temple dance with Halo Seronko.

Blaire Lindsay: Blaire-Lindsay.com
Support your awakening with this feminine embodiment coach.

THERAPEUTIC AND HEALING RESOURCES

FindAPsychologist.Org: FindAPsychologist.org
The American Psychological Association recommends this as a great resource to find a psychologist.

Hakomi: HakomiInstitute.com
A mindfulness-based, somatic psychotherapy method, the best method I know to hear your soul's voice in a safe, supported way.

Somatic Experiencing: TraumaHealing.org
For nervous system support, feeling your body, and self-regulation tools, try this "body-oriented therapeutic model that helps heal trauma and other stress disorders."

Family and Systemic Constellations: AllMyRelationsConstellations.com
A dynamic group work that utilizes the morphogenetic field of consciousness to bring healing. In my experience, the morphogenetic field is akin to the all-knowing womb of the Mother Goddess. Francesca Mason Boring is a great resource.

TRADITIONAL GODDESS PRACTICE GROUPS

For those looking to taste a divine feminine experience with traditional spiritual practice, I recommend:

Embody Shakti: EmbodyShakti.com

Nita Rubio is a lineage-holder from the Shri Vidya Tantra and Kashmiri Shaivism tradition, offering direct encounter with the Goddess through mantra, meditation, puja, and other traditional methodologies.

Anuttara Ashram: Anuttara.org

A nondual tantric ashram in northern British Columbia, Canada, which features traditional devotional practices for various forms in the Shakta Tantric tradition, supported by lineage teachings.

Satya Loka: SatyaLoka.net

International trainings and retreats in traditional Shakta Tantric practice, including yoga and devotional practices, supported by lineage teachings.

BOOKS

Awakening Shakti: The Transformative Power of the Goddesses of Yoga by Sally Kempton, et al. Wonderful work introducing the goddesses of India and how you can apply them to your life.

Conscious Femininity by Marion Woodman. A deep dive into understanding the feminine principle through Jungian analysis by one of the most revered experts on the topic.

When God Was a Woman by Merlin Stone, et al. A historical account of our ancient roots worshipping a female goddess, including how and why we lost it.

The Wild Woman's Way: Unlock Your Full Potential for Pleasure, Power, and Fulfillment by Michaela Boehm. This is a great resource to learn how to embody and experience pleasure throughout your life.

Women Who Run with the Wolves: Myths and Stories of the Wild Woman Archetype by Clarissa Pinkola Estés, PhD. Discover the power of the feminine archetype of the Wild Woman, through intercultural myths, fairy tales, folktales, etc.

OTHER RESOURCES

Nature Mandalas: AlishaFlecky.com/divinefemininemandalas
Discover and share your divine feminine nature mandalas with me.
For a deeper work on your sexuality:

Laura Carrotti: PathOfTantra.com
Laura Carrotti brings a punk rock heart to her 20 years of experience in tantra.

Homa and Mukto: HomaAndMukto.com
Homa and Mukto have been teaching together for over 30 years and are renowned meditation and neo-tantra teachers.

For support on money blocks and financial freedom:
Mar Michelle Hausler: GiveTakeLab.com

REFERENCES

Anasazi Foundation. *The Seven Paths: Changing One's Way of Walking in the World.* San Francisco: Berrett-Koehler Publishers, 2013.

Ardito, Mary. "Creativity: It's the Thought That Counts." *Bell Telephone Magazine* Volume 61, Issue 1, 1982.

Day, Dorothy. *The Long Loneliness: The Autobiography of the Legendary Catholic Social Activist.* San Francisco: HarperOne, 2017.

Estés, Clarissa Pinkola. *Women Who Run with the Wolves: Myths and Stories of the Wild Woman Archetype.* New York: Ballantine Books, 1995.

hooks, bell. *All About Love: New Visions.* New York: William Morrow Paperbacks, 2018.

Ladinsky, Daniel. *Love Poems from God: Twelve Sacred Voices from the East and West.* New York: Penguin Books, 2002.

Lal Ded. *I, Lalla: The Poems of Lal Ded* (Ranjit Hoskote, Trans.). New York: Penguin Classics, 2013. (Original work published ca. 14th century)

Lorde, Audre. *The Cancer Journals.* New York: Penguin Books, 2020.

Maathai, Wangari Muta. *Replenishing the Earth: Spiritual Values for Healing Ourselves and the World.* New York: Doubleday, 2010.

O'Donohue, John. *Anam Cara: A Book of Celtic Wisdom.* San Francisco: Harper Perennial, 2018.

"Pearl S. Buck." *New York Post,* April 26, 1959.

von Bingen, Hildegard. *Liber Scivias,* Graz: Akademische Druck-u. Verlagsanstalt. ND3385 H55 S279 2013. (Original work published 1151–1152).

Woodman, Marion. *Conscious Femininity* [Conference presentation]. "Our Time to Lead" Women & Power Conference, New York, NY. Sept. 10–13, 2004.

ACKNOWLEDGMENTS

The deepest acknowledgment I have and will always have is for the Divine Mother. I hope to honor this unnameable source of wisdom, meaning, beauty, and power with this book.

I recognize my teachers who guided me to taste frequencies of the divine feminine: Nita Rubio, Guruji Raj Kumar Baswar, Vajra Ma, Monika Nataraj, Paramita, Homa, Leela, and my mother.

Thank you to my partner and friends for your love, blessing, and support with this book. A special thanks to Joe Cho for his warmth and support.

This book is dedicated to Lakshmi.

ABOUT THE AUTHOR

ALISHA J. FLECKY is a somatic coach working with the Hakomi method and a facilitator of family/systemic constellations. She is a UCLA graduate and has an ecofriendly Bohemian clothing line. Alisha offers sacred feminine retreats and workshops internationally.

Alisha has been studying sacred feminine practices internationally since 2010. Her personal spiritual practice is with a Shri Vidya tantric lineage.

Alisha lives in the mountains of northern California with her partner, sister, many tall trees, and beloved friends and community. Discover more at AlishaFlecky.com.